A Call to the Miraculous

It's Time to Demonstrate the Power of God

Sean R. Pinder

"…my speech and my preaching was not with enticing words of man's wisdom, but in demonstration of the Spirit and of power…" 1 Corinthians 2:4

A Call to the Miraculous

It's Time to Demonstrate the Power of God

Unless otherwise indicated, all Scripture quotations are taken from the King James Version of the Bible.

Published by:
Sean R. Pinder
P.O. Box 117442, Carrollton, TX 75011-7442
info@miraclehealingcenter.net

Cover design by Jeffrey Zimmerman, Mark Zimmerman, and Valerie Zimmerman

ISBN: 978-06155604-9-6

Dedication

I dedicate this book to my wife, Aimee, the love of my life, my best friend, a Proverbs 31 woman, and the mother of my seven children. "Your children will rise up and call you blessed." You believed in me when hardly anyone else did. You stood by me during the toughest times in my walk with God. Days when I felt like throwing in the towel, God used you to encourage me not to quit. You are truly my precious gift from God. "Whoso findeth a wife findeth a good thing, and obtaineth favour of the LORD" (Proverbs 18:22). I thank God for you and, by God's grace, we will touch our generation with the love of God and the Gospel of Jesus Christ, followed by a demonstration of God's Miracle-Working Power.

Evangelists Sean and Aimee Pinder

Table of Contents

Part 1: A Call to the Miraculous

Part 2: Accounts of the Miraculous

**Both young and old alike are transformed by
the awesome power of God in every service.**

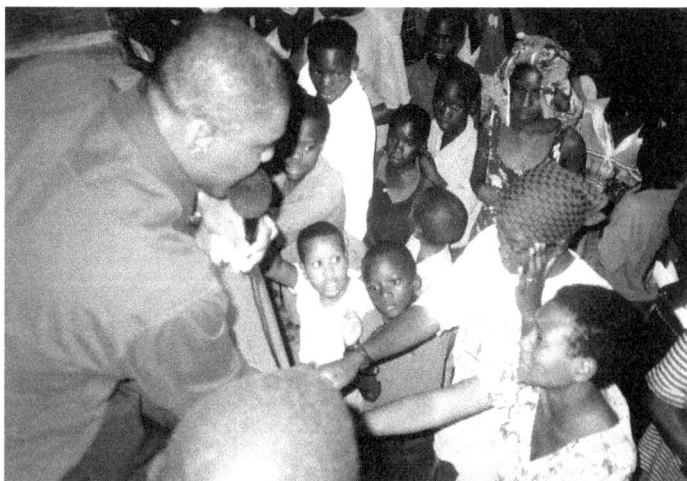

Part 1

A Call to the Miraculous

Pastors Sean and Aimee have brought God's saving and healing power to many.

Chapter 1
The Importance of Signs, Wonders, and Miracles in the Church

And my speech and my preaching was not with enticing words of man's wisdom, but in demonstration of the Spirit and of power: That your faith should not stand in the wisdom of men, but in the power of God (1Cor. 2:4-5).

When was the last time you saw a real healing miracle right before your eyes? This was the case as I preached at a church in Greensboro, North Carolina. I couldn't help but notice a man by the name of Gene who hobbled in on crutches with his wife next to him. I couldn't wait for the moment in the service for the healing power of God to touch His people. I preached a faith-building message from the Word of God concerning His healing power. The people's faith grasped every word.

Then the moment came to lay hands on the sick. I began to lay hands on Gene's leg brace and, as I did, a look of joy came on his face. With great excitement, Gene quickly began to loosen his leg brace with my help. By this time, every eye in the church was on Gene. He stood to his feet, unaided by his crutches, and began to stomp his feet on the ground. Next, he ran to the back of the church, and then to the front again, totally healed by the power of God. The entire church praised God for this great miracle of healing. Gene informed us that a 2000-pound paper bail had fallen on his leg at work and the doctor told him he would not be able to walk for three months. Thank God the doctor's report was changed.

The church, without signs, wonders, and miracles, falls short of operating in her fullest potential in Christ. The apostle Paul, under the Holy Ghost's inspiration, said,

> ... my speech and my preaching was not with enticing words of man's wisdom, but in demonstration of the Spirit and of power: that your faith should not stand in the wisdom of man but in the power of God (1 Cor. 2:4, 5).

Miracles must be demonstrated so that the body of Christ can have a real, living faith that causes an impact against the powers of darkness. According to this Scripture, did you notice where God desires our faith to be? "... In the power of God..."

Today, too many of our church pulpits are overwhelmed with preaching man-made wisdom and enticing words. Most of the church's faith is in good preaching. Simply put, this kind of preaching tells people what they want to hear and not what they need to hear. No wonder there is a lack of changed lives. Some of the church's faith is in the wrong place. Year after year, thousands gather and pay to go to conferences all around the world to hear how they are going to be blessed. Disappointed, they return again to homes of poverty, lack, and sickness because their faith is in man's wisdom and not in God's power. The apostle Paul said, "For the preaching of the cross is to them that perish foolishness; but unto us which are saved it is the power of God" (1 Cor. 1:18).

Miracles in the church are not optional. The Lord's command applies to the church in every generation. Consider Mark 16:15-18:

> 15 And he said unto them, Go ye into all the world, and preach the gospel to every creature.
> 16 He that believeth and is baptized shall be saved; but he that believeth not shall be damned.
> 17 And these signs shall follow them that believe; in my name shall they cast out devils; they shall speak with new tongues;
> 18 They shall take up serpents; and if they drink any deadly thing, it shall not hurt them; they shall lay hands on the sick, and they shall recover.

Notice three things that Christ commanded the Church before He ascended into heaven:

1. Go into all the world.
2. Preach the Gospel to every creature.
3. And these signs shall follow them that believe.

This simply means, wherever we go in this world and preach the Gospel, signs should follow. Jesus did not say these signs might follow. He said firmly, "…these signs shall follow them that believe…" Later, in the same chapter, the disciples demonstrated that they understood the Lord's command. "…And they [the disciples] went forth, and preached everywhere, the Lord working with them, and confirming the word with signs following…" (Mark 16:20).

God's manifested miraculous power causes the church to grow rapidly. When miracles take place, people come to church services with great expectation. Their faith is alive. The book of Acts demonstrates this perfectly in Acts 5:12-16:

12 And by the hands of the apostles were many signs and wonders wrought among the people; (and they were all with one accord in Solomon's porch.
13 And of the rest durst no man join

himself to them: but the people magnified them.

14 And believers were the more added to the Lord, multitudes both of men and women.)

15 Insomuch that they brought forth the sick into the streets, and laid them on beds and couches, that at the least the shadow of Peter passing by might overshadow some of them.

16 There came also a multitude out of the cities round about unto Jerusalem, bringing sick folks, and them which were vexed with unclean spirits: and they were healed every one.

The Holy Spirit gives key elements in these passages of Scripture that we can glean from and get Bible results. As a result of signs and wonders by the apostles' hands, the Scriptures say, "…the people magnified them." The church reverenced the apostles because they could not deny that God was with them. Undeniable signs and wonders were evident in their midst. These miracles gave the people a personal point of reference concerning all the Scriptures they were ever taught. The Bible became alive. They no longer heard and had faith by just hearing the Word, but now their faith was strengthened because they saw the evidence. They now had proof of the Gospel.

In our own ministry, we planned a crusade in Uganda, Africa. Before our arrival, we publicized the services through fliers, posters, radio commercials, and involvement from the local churches. The week we arrived, we had a parade with a sound system used to encourage those in the area to attend. A lady who had a paralyzed foot lived near the crusade grounds. She was well informed about the event, yet neither she nor her children made any effort to come.

She did not come because she was used to hearing the preached Word without a demonstration of miracles. Her house was so close to the crusade grounds that she could hear the service and the message being preached. While listening, her faith was ignited and she, too, received a miracle from God. God Himself demonstrated to her His mighty power by healing her paralyzed foot. Her foot was made whole and she walked without any assistance. That night, she came to the evening service to testify of what God had done in her life. She came out of her house because she now saw God in action.

The church grew as a result of miracles. "And believers were the more added to the Lord, MULTITUDES both of men and women. Insomuch that they brought forth the sick..." Look at Acts 3:1-9:

> 1 Now Peter and John went up together into the temple at the hour of prayer, being the ninth hour.

14

2 And a certain man lame from his mother's womb was carried, whom they laid daily at the gate of the temple which is called Beautiful, to ask alms of them that entered into the temple;

3 Who seeing Peter and John about to go into the temple asked alms.

4 And Peter, fastening his eyes upon him with John, said, Look on us.

5 And he gave heed unto them, expecting to receive something of them.

6 Then Peter said, Silver and gold have I none; but such as I have give I thee: In the name of Jesus Christ of Nazareth rise up and walk.

7 And he took him by the right hand, and lifted him up: and immediately his feet and ankle bones received strength.

8 And he leaping up stood, and walked, and entered with them into the temple, walking, and leaping, and praising God.

9 And all the people saw him walking and praising God.

The result of the miracle of healing this man lame from birth was "… many of them which heard the word believed; and the number of the men was about five thousand" (Acts 4:4).

One miraculous demonstration instantly drew five thousand men into God's kingdom.

Miraculous demonstrations can do more than a thousand sermons. Could this be the reason for the lack of growth in many churches? This is God's original design to convert the world. The apostle Paul, under the inspiration of the Holy Ghost, confirmed this when he said,

> For I will not dare to speak of any of those things which Christ hath not wrought by me, to make the Gentiles obedient, by word and deed, through mighty signs and wonders, by the power of the Spirit of God; so that from Jerusalem, and round about unto Illyricum, I have fully preached the gospel of Christ (Rom. 15:18-19).

God's power draws people from every type of background. In an atmosphere of miracles, people's needs are met both spiritually and physically. The life of God is manifested. No wonder some churches are stagnant and cannot grow. There is no life of God. The church is dead and faith is dead because "…faith without works is dead…" (James 2:26).

When faith is alive, ministers don't beg believers to invite their family and friends to church. People gladly bring family members and friends

16

because they know God's power is going to manifest, their needs will be met, and lives will be changed. As a church, we must repent and go back to God's original plan of preaching the Gospel of Jesus Christ that is followed by a demonstration of miracles.

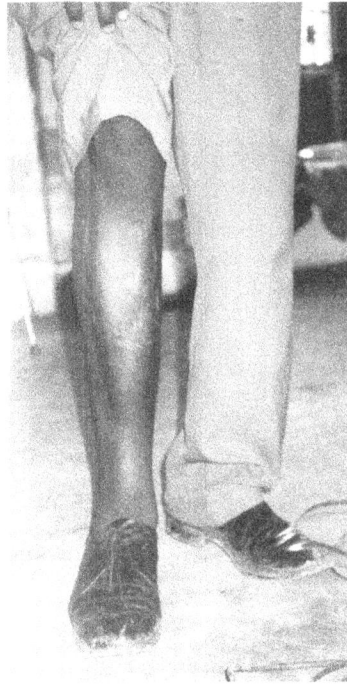

After suffering with cancer for twelve years in his right leg, this man was healed during a miracle crusade in Uganda, Africa.

Evangelist Sean Pinder

Chapter 2
Miracles Follow the Preaching of the Gospel

My wife and I often grieve over the fact that many people don't even preach Christ and Him crucified. Could this be one of the many reasons for the lack of miracle-working power that opens blind eyes, unstops deaf ears, and makes cripples walk? Examine closely the Biblical accounts of what took place when the true Gospel was preached. From a review of these Scriptures, it is evident that, whenever the true Gospel is preached, miracles follow. Read the following four passages:

- 20 And they went forth, and preached [the Gospel] everywhere, the Lord working with them, and confirming the word with signs following. Amen (Mark 16:20).

- 1 Then he called his twelve disciples together, and gave them power and authority over all devils, and to cure diseases.
  2 And he sent them to preach the

kingdom of God, and to heal the sick.
And they departed, and went through the towns, preaching the gospel, and healing everywhere (Luke 9:1, 2, 6)

- 5 Then Philip went down to the city of Samaria, and preached Christ unto them.
6 And the people with one accord gave heed unto those things which Philip spake, hearing and seeing the miracles which he did.
7 For unclean spirits, crying with loud VOICE came out of many that were possessed with them: and many taken with palsies, and that were lame, were healed.
8 And there was great joy in that city (Acts 8:5-8).

- 3 Long time therefore abode they speaking [preaching the gospel] boldly in the Lord, which gave testimony unto the word of his grace, and granted signs and wonders to be done by their hands (Acts 14:3).

Do you see the pattern? Every time the apostles, evangelists, and deacons in the early church preached the Gospel, demonstrations followed.

In this generation, we hardly hear any preaching on repentance or the death, burial, and resurrection of the Lord Jesus Christ. When examined closely, one cannot help but realize that the Lord only confirms the Gospel of Jesus Christ. No wonder the apostle Paul said, "For I am not ashamed of the gospel of Christ: for it is the power of God unto salvation to everyone that believeth..."

I can feel the Holy Ghost as I type this manuscript. God's heart cries for some preachers to stop preaching a man-made, fleshly, half-hearted message and to preach the uncompromised Gospel of Jesus Christ. Then, and only then, will we see a true demonstration of God's power to heal the sick, open blind eyes, unstop deaf ears, cause cripples to walk, and raise the dead. How my heart yearns within me to see Jesus in action the way He was in the disciples' lives. A call is going out from God's heart to those who are listening and willing to respond to seek God's face for the miraculous. We must get back to God's original plan. We need to preach the Gospel in the Holy Ghost's power followed by an outpouring of miracles.

Throw away big, fancy words and impressive preaching. Enticing words do not produce real faith that brings about a genuine change. Get back to uncompromised preaching that confronts sin such as adultery, fornication, lying, stealing, hatred, envy, jealousy, etc. I have come to a place in God where it is my heart's desire to please Him above all. The apostle Paul said,

> For Christ sent me not to baptize, but to preach the gospel: not with wisdom of words, lest the cross of Christ should be made of none effect. For the preaching of the cross is to them that perish foolishness; but unto us which are saved it is the power of God (1 Cor. 1:17-18).

I refuse to believe that God has placed His precious Holy Spirit upon us just to talk about things that do not pertain to the preaching of the Gospel. The anointing is not for us to win a popularity contest. Jesus made the purpose of the anointing upon His life clear.

> The Spirit of the Lord is upon me, because he hath anointed me to preach the gospel to the poor; he hath sent me to heal the brokenhearted, to preach deliverance to the captives, and recovering of sight to the blind, to set at liberty them that are bruised, To preach the acceptable year of the Lord (Luke 4:18-19).

Preaching the whole Gospel includes a demonstration of signs, wonders, and miracles. You cannot separate the two. God never intended anyone to preach without a demonstration. Anytime the Lord mentions the command to preach the Gospel, He never fails to include the miraculous.

We must examine our preaching and:

> ...dare not make ourselves of the number, or compare ourselves with some that commend themselves: but they measuring themselves by themselves, and comparing themselves among themselves, are not wise (2 Cor. 10:12).

It is vital to look closely at God's Word to see how Jesus and the apostles preached the Gospel and to follow their pattern. We must preach and demonstrate.

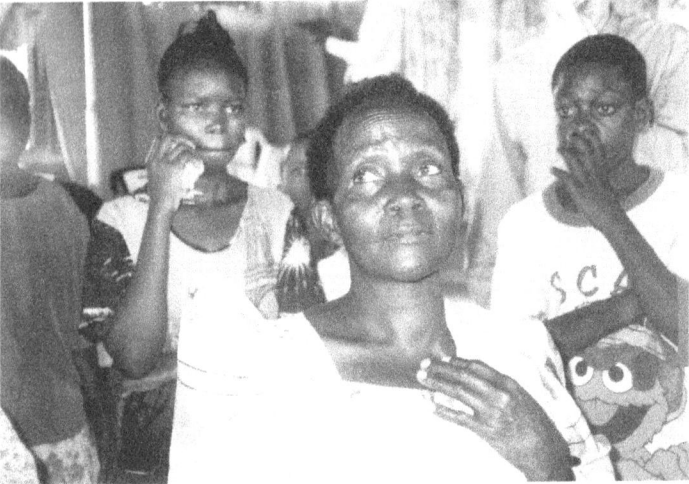

This woman had a grapefruit-sized tumor in her stomach. After the laying on of hands, God caused it to vanish.

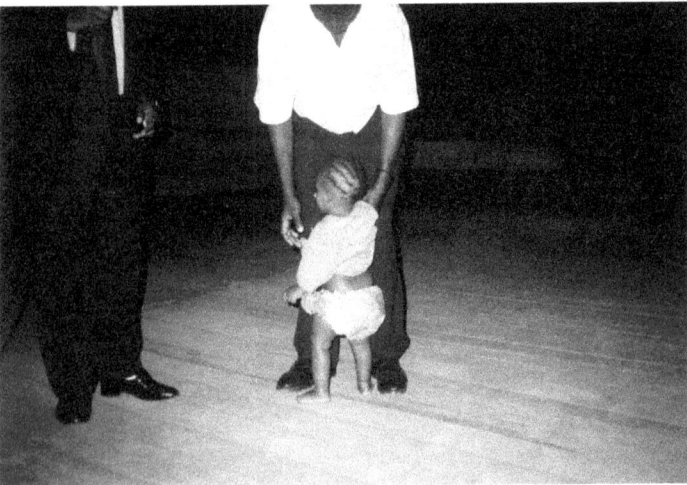

This baby's legs were paralyzed so that he could not stand. After the prayer of faith, he was totally healed and now can walk perfectly.

Chapter 3
Approved by Signs, Wonders, and Miracles

Insomuch that the multitude wondered, when they saw the dumb to speak, the maimed to be whole, the lame to walk, and the blind to see: and they glorified the God of Israel (Matt. 15:31).

Miraculous signs following the preaching of the Gospel are God's approval that Jesus Christ is God's Son and that He rose from the dead on the third day. God's Word declares this truth. The Bible is not man's opinions or ideas; it is the infallible, incorruptible Word of the Living God who abides forever. "All scripture is given by inspiration of God..." (2 Tim. 3:16). Concerning God's approval of signs, wonders, and miracles, God's Word states, "Ye men of Israel, hear these words; Jesus of Nazareth, a man approved of God among you by miracles and wonders and signs, which God did by him in the midst of you, as ye yourselves also know..." (Acts 2:22). In this particular passage of Scripture mentioned, the word "approved" in the Greek means "to accredit"[1]; "to recommend"; "to vouch for."[2] It is

---

1 Strong's Concordance of the Bible
2 Ibid

such an honor to know that the God of heaven and earth vouches for His children and backs up what they are saying by miraculous signs.

Jesus is God's Son. If He had to be approved of God by the supernatural demonstration, what makes preachers today think they do not need God's approval of their preaching in this same manner? Jesus made a strong statement when He said, "...as my Father hath sent me, even so send I you" (John 20:21). How did God send Jesus? Jesus Himself explains,

> The Spirit of the Lord is upon me, because he hath anointed me to preach the gospel to the poor; he hath sent me to heal the brokenhearted, to preach deliverance to the captives, and recovering of sight to the blind, to set at liberty them that are bruised... (Luke 4:18-19).

God did not send Jesus without any power to demonstrate.

John the Baptist was shut up in prison, became discouraged, and began to doubt that Jesus was the promised Messiah. To overcome his doubt, John sent some of His disciples to ask Jesus this question, "...Art thou he that should come? Or do we look for another?" (Luke 7:20).

And in that same hour he cured many of their infirmities and plagues, and of evil spirits; and unto many that were blind he gave sight. Then Jesus answering said unto them, Go your way, and tell John what things ye have seen and heard; how that the blind see, the lame walk, the lepers are cleansed, the deaf hear, the dead are raised, to the poor the gospel is preached. And blessed is he, whosoever shall not be offended in me (Luke 7:21-23).

Jesus did not give John a nice, long, impressive answer. He got right to the point, demonstrated the power of God, and then told John's disciples, "…Go and shew John again those things which ye do hear and see..."

Nicodemus, a spiritual leader in Israel, had to confess to Jesus and say, "…we know that thou art a teacher come from God: for no man can do these miracles that thou doest, except God be with him" (John 3:2). Nicodemus was compelled to realize that Jesus was approved by God because he himself saw the miracles that Jesus performed.

Jesus did not preach without a demonstration. He is the perfect will of God in action. Should we expect to do less than Jesus did? Jesus is the standard and the one whom we should all pattern ourselves after. Jesus made a bold and profound statement under the Holy Ghost's anointing when He said, "But I have greater witness than that of John: for the works which the Father hath given me to finish, the same works that I do, bear witness of me, that the Father hath sent me" (John 5:36). The works Jesus referred to in this passage were signs, wonders, and miracles. They were proof that God sent Him.

Some of the religious leaders were the worst enemies of the apostles in the book of Acts. They tried to shut the mouths of Peter and John. They intensely hated the apostles because God worked mightily through them to preach Christ's Gospel and heal the sick. The apostles' enemies confessed, "…What shall we do to these men? For that indeed a notable miracle hath been done by them is manifest to all them that dwell in Jerusalem; and we cannot deny it" (Acts 4:16). I pray to God that the enemies of today's true disciples would say the same thing.

Moses was chosen as God's messenger to deliver the children of Israel. After God had appeared to Moses and commissioned him, Moses made strong proposals to God that every man and woman of God should also make. Look at Exodus 4:1-9:

> 1 And Moses answered and said, But, behold, they will not believe me, nor hearken unto my voice: for they will say, The LORD hath not appeared unto thee.

2 And the LORD said unto him, What is that in thine hand? And he said, A rod.

3 And he said, Cast it on the ground. And he cast it on the ground, and it became a serpent; and Moses fled from before it.

4 And the LORD said unto Moses, Put forth thine hand, and take it by the tail. And he put forth his hand, and caught it, and it became a rod in his hand:

5 That they may believe that the LORD God of their fathers, the God of Abraham, the God of Isaac, and the God of Jacob, hath appeared unto thee.

6 And the LORD said furthermore unto him, Put now thine hand into thy bosom. And he put his hand into his bosom: and when he took it out, behold, his hand was leprous as snow.

7 And he said, Put thine hand into thy bosom again. And he put his hand into his bosom again; and plucked it out of his bosom, and, behold, it was turned again as his other flesh.

8 And it shall come to pass, if they will not believe thee, neither hearken to the voice of the first sign, that they will believe the voice of the latter sign.

9 And it shall come to pass, if they will

not believe also these two signs, neither hearken unto thy voice, that thou shalt take of the water of the river, and pour it upon the dry land: and the water which thou takest out of the river shall become blood upon the dry land.

According to these Scriptures, miracles have a voice.

Notice closely how God said, "...the voice of the first sign...the voice of the latter sign." The miraculous is God's voice testifying and giving confirmation on behalf of His messenger. Moses had to have the miraculous demonstration in the people's sight as evidence that God had appeared to him.

Let's look at the people's reaction once the message Moses delivered was confirmed with the miraculous.

And Moses and Aaron went and gathered together all the elders of the children of Israel: And Aaron spake all the words which the LORD had spoken unto Moses, and did the signs in the sight of the people. And the people believed: and when they heard that the LORD had visited the children of Israel, and that he had looked upon their affliction, then they bowed their heads and worshipped (Ex. 4:29-31).

God hasn't changed this principle. He told Moses to perform the miracles in the people's sight "that they may believe that the LORD God of their fathers, the God of Abraham, the God of Isaac, and the God of Jacob, hath appeared unto thee."

Another Old Testament example where we see this same principle at work is in the life of the prophet Elijah. Elijah confronted the people of Israel. They had turned their backs on God and worshipped the god by the name of Baal. Elijah confronted them saying, "...How long halt ye between two opinions? If the LORD be God, follow him: but if Baal, then follow him. And the people answered him not a word" (1 Kings 18:27). The people did not respond to the Lord's Word spoken by Elijah.

Now let us go a step further. After the Word was confirmed with a miraculous demonstration, the people reacted. The Scripture says,

> And it came to pass at the time of the offering of the evening sacrifice, that Elijah the prophet came near, and said, LORD God of Abraham, Isaac, and of Israel, let it be known this day that thou art God in Israel, and that I am thy servant. and that I have done all these things at thy word. Hear me, O LORD, hear me, that this people may know that thou art the LORD God. and that thou

31

hast turned their heart back again. Then
the fire of the LORD fell, and consumed
the burnt sacrifice, and the wood, and the
stones, and the dust, and licked up the
water that was in the trench. And when
all the people saw it, they fell on their
faces: and they said, The LORD, he is the
God; the LORD, he is the God.

Do you see it now? God's Word says, "…when
all the people saw it, they fell on their faces: and they
said, The LORD, he is the God…" They saw God's
servant's message confirmed by a miraculous sign.
No one could deny that God had sent Elijah and that
his message was directly from God. One
demonstration brought all the people to their knees,
confessing "the Lord He is God" (I Kings 18: 36-39).

I remember a miracle crusade we held in
Uganda, Africa a few years ago. As I preached the
Gospel during the first service, I received tough looks
from the pastors and those attending. The Holy Ghost
was upon me in a powerful way to preach. But the
looks on the people's faces told me they needed proof
to accompany the Word.

I called for those to come forward who needed
healing in their bodies. The blind, deaf, demon-
possessed, and diseased came forward. People
watched intensely to see if anything was going to
happen. I prayed for a nine-year-old boy who was

born deaf in his right ear. Putting my finger in his right ear, I commanded the spirit of deafness to come out of the boy in the name of Jesus. Afterwards, I had the interpreter check his right ear. To everyone's amazement, including the interpreter's, the boy could now hear perfectly in his once deaf right ear.

All of a sudden, faith came alive and many more people with ailments and diseases began to come forward. God responds to faith. The next miracle that took place was a woman, who was totally blind in one eye and going blind in the other eye, receiving sight. Tumors the size of grapefruits began to vanish out of others. A young fifteen-year-old demon-possessed girl was totally set free and gave her heart to Jesus.

All of these things took place during the morning service. Everyone's tough looks had vanished and were replaced by smiles and great rejoicing. The people could not deny that God was there when He demonstrated His miracles. "…This gospel of the kingdom shall be preached in all the world for a witness unto all nations; and then shall the end come" (Matt. 24:14). The word "witness" in the Greek means "something evidential,"[3] or "evidence given."[4] Jesus commanded us to preach the Gospel to all the nations with evidence.

The Bible says in Acts 1:3, "…he (Jesus)

---

3 Ibid
4 Ibid

shewed himself alive after his passion by many infallible proofs…" Jesus is still the same and, if He is, miracles ought to follow everywhere His servants go and proclaim the Gospel's truth. Miracles prove that Jesus is alive and they are God's way of placing His stamp of approval on Gospel preaching.

The book of Hebrews 2:4 says, "God also bearing them witness, both with signs and WONDERS and with divers miracles, and gifts of the Holy Ghost, according to his own will…" The words "bearing them witness…", in the Greek, mean "to testify further jointly; i.e., unite in adding evidence."[5] What an honor to know that the King of heaven and earth unites with us, adding evidence to the message of the Gospel.

---

5 Ibid

Chapter 4
The Purpose of Miracles in the Life of Christ

Jesus is our perfect example of how to
accomplish God's will. Without miracles in Christ's
life, He would not have drawn the multitudes. If our
ministering the Gospel is to be successful, we must do
things the way Jesus did. In the Gospel of John, we
have a strong testimony from an apostle who was a
direct eyewitness to Jesus' ministry. Listen to John's
words, "And a great multitude followed him, because
they saw his miracles which he did on them that were
diseased" (John 6:2). The multitude came because
God's power was demonstrated right before their
eyes. We must follow Christ's example to have
successful ministries.

"Then many of the Jews which came to Mary,
and had seen the things which Jesus did, believed on
Him" (John 11:45). Here, God reveals His ultimate
purpose for raising Lazarus from the dead. God
worked miracles through Christ so the Jews could
believe on Him and be saved. Concerning Lazarus,
Jesus declared, "…This sickness is not unto death, but
for the glory of God, that the Son of God might be
glorified thereby" (John 11:4). How was Jesus

glorified? He was glorified when many believed in Him after seeing the miracle of raising Lazarus from the dead. These Scriptures and many more reveal the purpose of miracles in Christ's life.

In order for the disciples to have a living faith in Jesus Christ, He performed miracles. The Bible clearly says, "This beginning of miracles did Jesus in Cana of Galilee, and manifested forth his glory; and his disciples believed on him" (John 2:11). "Jesus Christ the same yesterday, and today, and forever" (Hebrews 13:8). Jesus did not change. Christ's present-day disciples must see miracles as the twelve disciples did if they are going to have a real, living faith in Jesus, who is alive forever.

Jesus challenged the very core of the religious system of His day. The Pharisees and the Sadducees loved ceremonies, rituals, and the praise of men rather than the praise of God. They loved their titles, positions, and long robes to be seen of men while they pretended to be something they weren't. In God's eyes, they were nothing more than a sounding brass and a tinkling cymbal. They were angry at Jesus and wanted to stone him.

Despite the opposition, Jesus said, "If I do not the works of my Father believe me not. But if I do, though ye believe not me, believe the works: that ye may know, and believe, that the Father is in me, and I in him" (John 10:37-38). Jesus never expected people to believe His message unless there was a demonstration of the miraculous. Jesus dealt with the religious leaders' challenges. The religious leaders were determined to do away with Jesus. He had worked so many miracles that multitudes accepted Him and believed He was the Messiah. The leaders were jealous because He demonstrated power they did not have. The people said, "What a word is this! For with authority and power he commandeth the unclean spirits, and they come out" (Luke 4:36).

On one occasion, Jesus had forgiven a sick man's sins. This act had brought on much persecution by the scribes and Pharisees. Outraged at Christ's mercy, they said, "...Who is this which speaketh blasphemies? Who can forgive sins, but God alone?" (Luke 5:21). Christ's power to forgive sins was put into question. I love the way Christ responded to His critics. No long discussion or discourse occurred. Actions speak louder than words. Jesus answered firmly and demonstrated.

> Whether is easier, to say, Thy sins be forgiven thee; or to say, Rise up and walk? But that ye may know that the Son of man hath power upon earth to forgive sins, (he said unto the sick of the palsy,) I say unto thee, Arise, and take up thy couch, and go into thine house. And immediately he rose up before them, and took up that whereon he lay, and departed

> to his own house, glorifying God. And
> they were all amazed, and they glorified
> God, and were filled with fear, saying, we
> have seen strange things to day (Luke
> 5:23-26).

Jesus' healing of the palsy forever settled the question of Christ's authority on earth to forgive sins.

Miracles reveal the Lord's mercy and compassion.

> And they came to Jericho: and as he went
> out of Jericho with his disciples and a
> great number of people, blind Bartimaeus,
> the son of Timaeus, sat by the highway
> side begging. And when he heard that it
> was Jesus of Nazareth, he began to cry
> out, and say, Jesus, thou Son of David,
> have mercy on me" (Mark 10:46-47).

How did Jesus respond to this cry for mercy? "And Jesus stood still, and commanded him to be called" (Mark 10:49). What happened next changed Bartimaeus' life forever.

> And Jesus answered and said unto him,
> What wilt thou that I should do unto thee?
> The blind man said unto him, Lord, that I
> might receive my sight. And Jesus said
> unto him, Go thy way; thy faith hath

made thee whole. And immediately he received his sight, and followed Jesus in the way (Mark 10:51-52).

Blind Bartimaeus asked Jesus to have mercy on him. Jesus demonstrated His mercy by healing Bartimaeus' blind eyes.

Jesus reveals powerful principles in Scripture concerning how He ministered. I admire Jesus more than any man on the planet. I love how simple, yet profound, He functioned in ministry. We are without excuse. Christ powerfully stated, "Verily, verily, I say unto you, He that believeth on me, the works that I do shall he do also; and greater works than these shall he do; because I go unto my Father" (John 14:12). Here are some of the many Scriptures that show us the way Christ ministered:

- 23 And Jesus went about all Galilee, teaching in their synagogues, and preaching the gospel of the kingdom, and healing all manner of sickness and all manner of disease among the 24 And his fame went throughout all Syria: and they brought unto him all sick people that were taken with divers diseases and torments, and those which were possessed with devils, and those which were

lunatick, and those that had the palsy; and he healed them.
25 And there followed him great multitudes of people from Galilee, and from Decapolis, and from Jerusalem, and from Judea, and from beyond Jordan (Matt. 4:23-25).

- 35 And Jesus went about all the cities and villages, teaching in their synagogues, and preaching the gospel of the kingdom, and healing every sickness and every disease among the people.
36 But when he saw the multitudes, he was moved with compassion on them, because they fainted, and were scattered abroad, as sheep having no shepherd (Matt. 9:35-36).

- 29 And Jesus departed from thence, and came nigh unto the sea of Galilee; and went up into a mountain, and sat down there.
30 And great multitudes came unto him, having with them those that were lame, blind, dumb, maimed,

and many others, and cast them down at Jesus' feet; and he healed them:

31 Insomuch that the multitude wondered, when they saw the dumb to speak, the maimed to be whole, the lame to walk, and the blind to see: and they glorified the God of Israel (Matt. 15:29-31).

- 32 And they bring unto him one that was deaf, and had an impediment in his speech; and they beseech him to put his hand upon him.

33 And he took him aside from the multitude, and put his fingers into his ears, and he spit, and touched his tongue;

34 And looking up to heaven, he sighed, and saith unto him, Ephphatha, that is, Be opened.

35 And straightway his ears were opened, and the string of his tongue was loosed, and he spake plain.

36 And he charged them that they should tell no man: but the more he charged them, so much the more a great deal they published it;

37 And were beyond measure astonished, saying, He hath done all things well: he maketh both the deaf to hear, and the dumb to speak (Mark 7:32-37).

- 14 And Jesus returned in the power of the Spirit into Galilee: and there went a fame of him through all the region round about.
15 And he taught in their synagogues, being glorified of all.
16 And he came to Nazareth, where he had been brought up: and as his custom was, he went into the synagogue on the sabbath day, and stood up for to read.
17 And there was delivered unto him the book of the prophet Esaias. And when he had opened the book, he found the place where it was written,
18 The Spirit of the Lord is upon me, because he hath anointed me to preach the gospel to the poor; he hath sent me to heal the brokenhearted, to preach

deliverance to the captives, and recovering of sight to the blind, to set at liberty them that are bruised, 19 To preach the acceptable year of the Lord (Luke 4:14-19).

- 32 And they were astonished at his doctrine: for his word was with power.
33 And in the synagogue there was a man, which had a spirit of an unclean devil, and cried out with a loud voice,
34 Saying, Let us alone; what have we to do with thee, thou Jesus of Nazareth? art thou come to destroy us? I know thee who thou art; the Holy One of God.
35 And Jesus rebuked him, saying, Hold thy peace, and come out of him. And when the devil had thrown him in the midst, he came out of him, and hurt him not.
36 And they were all amazed, and spake among themselves, saying, What a word is this! for with authority and power he commandeth the unclean spirits, and they come out (Luke 4:32-36).

- 40 Now when the sun was setting, all they that had any sick with divers diseases brought them unto him; and he laid his hands on every one of them, and healed them.
41 And devils also came out of many, crying out, and saying, Thou art Christ the Son of God. And he rebuking them suffered them not to speak: for they knew that he was Christ (Luke 4:40-41).

- 17 And he came down with them, and stood in the plain, and the company of his disciples, and a great multitude of people out of all Judaea and Jerusalem, and from the sea coast of Tyre and Sidon, which came to hear him, and to be healed of their diseases;
18 And they that were vexed with unclean spirits: and they were healed.
19 And the whole multitude sought to touch him: for there went virtue [POWER] out of him, and healed them all (Luke 6:17-19).

Jesus ministered as a man anointed by the Holy Ghost. He perfectly exemplifies how ministry must be done. The apostle Peter said these words about Jesus: "How God anointed Jesus of Nazareth with the Holy Ghost and with power: who went about doing good, and healing all that were oppressed of the devil; for God was with him" (Acts 10:38). Jesus taught, preached, and then healed. Jesus did not just talk about the Kingdom of God, He demonstrated it. As Christ's ministers, we must follow His example of preaching and demonstrating.

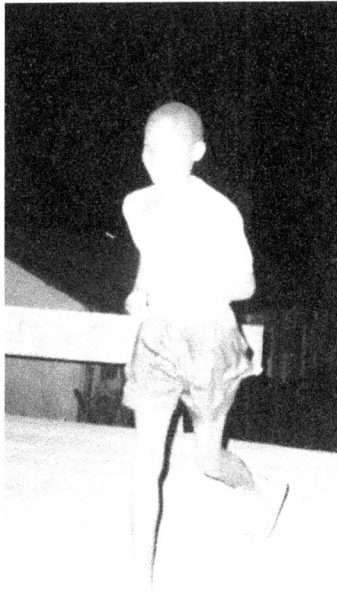

This boy came to the Uganda Crusade with a broken leg. He left running, leaping, and praising God.

Evangelist Sean Pinder

Chapter 5
Reasons the Church Today Lacks the Miraculous

In order to understand the reasons for the lack of the miraculous, we must go to God's Word. "For the word of the LORD is right…" (Psalms 33:4). In the book of Matthew, the seventeenth chapter, God's Word shines much light on this subject.

> And when they were come to the multitude, there came to him a certain man, kneeling down to him, and saying, Lord, have mercy on my son: for he is lunatick, and sore vexed: for ofttimes he falleth into the fire, and oft into the water. And I brought him to thy disciples, and they could not cure him (Matt. 17:14-16).

What a serious charge this is against the church! The King of kings and Lord of lords responded, "O faithless and perverse generation, how long shall I be with you? How long shall I suffer you? Bring him hither to me" (Matt. 17:17). Jesus strongly rebuked the church. Jesus said that His disciples were FAITHLESS and PERVERSE. "Faithless" means "unbelieving"[6] and "perverse" means "corrupt."[7] How do we know that Jesus was talking to the disciples? Later on in the same chapter, the disciples came "...to Jesus apart [privately], and said, Why could not we cast him out? And Jesus said unto them, Because of your unbelief..." (Matt. 17:19-20). Unbelief and corruption are major causes for the lack of God's power being manifested in many churches.

Jesus did not just talk about unbelief, but He also mentioned the word "perverse." Some people don't want preachers to talk about sin anymore. Jesus does. Perverse means corrupt. Today, most preachers are afraid to confront the church's corruption. We hardly hear preaching on lying, gossiping, jealousy, stealing, cheating, fornication, adultery, gambling, etc. Jesus said the lack of miracles is also caused by a church that is steeped in sin.

Sound doctrine is not desired by most churches today. They just want a good shouting time with preaching that does not require change. The preaching of the Cross is being less heard by their congregations. The apostle Paul said,

> For the time will come when they will not endure sound doctrine; but after their own lusts shall they heap to them-

---

6 Ibid
7 Ibid

selves teachers, having itching ears; And they shall turn away their ears from the truth, and shall be turned unto fables (2 Tim. 4:3-4).

The lack of God's Word being preached is also the cause for the lack of the miraculous. The Bible says, "And they went forth, and preached everywhere, the Lord working with them, and confirming the word with signs following" (Mark 16:20). The Lord only confirms His Word.

In the church today, most don't realize that the supernatural healing of the sick is a command. The book of Ezekiel reveals that God had serious issues with the preachers for not healing His people. God reveals His heart concerning His shepherds,

...The word of the LORD came unto me, saying, Son of man, prophesy against the shepherds of Israel, prophesy, and say unto them, Thus saith the Lord GOD unto the shepherds; Woe be to the shepherds of Israel that do feed themselves! Should not the shepherds feed the flocks? Ye eat the fat, and ye clothe you with the wool, ye kill them that are fed: but ye feed not the flock. The diseased have ye not strengthened, neither have ye healed that which was sick, neither have ye bound up that which was broken, neither have ye brought again that which was driven away, neither have ye sought that which was lost; but with force and with cruelty have ye ruled them. And they were scattered, because there is no shepherd: and they became meat to all the beasts of the field, when they were scattered (Ez. 34:1-5).

God expects His ministers to heal the sick and cast out devils. It is the Gospel of Jesus Christ.

In most circles today, the miraculous is hardly ever taught to people. The Bible states, "So then faith cometh by hearing, and hearing by the word of God" (Rom. 10:17). In order for people to grasp the truth of signs, wonders, and miracles, preachers are obligated to preach the revelation of the miraculous. The Word also declares, "My people are destroyed for lack of knowledge: because thou hast rejected knowledge…" (Hos. 4:6).

I love the simplicity of Christ's preaching. He did not only talk about the problem, but he also presented the solution: "Howbeit this kind goeth not out but by prayer and fasting" (Matt. 17:21). In the Scripture mentioned, the lack of prayer and fasting results in no miracles. In the following chapter, we will discuss what steps the church must take to tap into the supernatural miracle-working power of God.

A metal gate fell on this New Orleans man, crushing his spine, forcing doctors to fuse it at three levels. After his healing, he demonstrated by jumping, by stretching, and by touching his toes.

This woman depended on her cane to walk. One encounter with God's miraculous power, and she no longer needed the cane.

After a stroke, this lady had to walk with a cane. Now, she stands in amazement as Evangelist Sean holds the cane up high for all to see God has healed her.

Chapter 6
The Price for the Miraculous

Again, the kingdom of heaven is like unto treasure hid in a field; the which when a man hath found, he hideth, and for joy thereof goeth and selleth all that he hath, and buyeth that field.
Again, the kingdom of heaven is like unto a merchant man, seeking goodly pearls: Who, when he had found one pearl of great price, went and sold all that he had, and bought it (Matt. 13:44-46).

Nothing of great value comes easy. God's Word reveals the necessary steps we must take in preparing to be a conduit of God's power. Look at Jesus, who is the Living Word, and follow Him. He said, "I am the way, the truth, and the life..." (John 14:6). Jesus is the way to God's power. Jesus also gives us a strong instruction when He says, "...He that believeth on me, the works that I do shall he do also..." (John 14:12).

I remember, when I first came across this Bible verse, I was amazed. I never dreamed that it was possible that anyone who believes could do the works of Christ. Let us closely examine the verse. "...The works that I do shall he do also..." What were the first works of Christ that enabled God's miracle-working power to flow through Him? These Scriptures reveal His first works. "And Jesus being full of the Holy Ghost returned from Jordan, and was led by the Spirit into the wilderness, being forty days tempted of the devil. And in those days he did eat nothing: and when they were ended, he afterward hungered" (Luke 4:1-2).

These Scriptures indicate that one of Jesus' first works was an extended forty-day fast. The answer Christ gave His disciples explains the purpose of His long fast.

> ...If ye have faith as a grain of mustard seed, ye shall say unto this mountain, Remove hence to yonder place; and it shall remove; and nothing shall be impossible unto you. Howbeit this kind goeth not out but by prayer and fasting (Matt. 17:20-21).

Christ's fast resulted in power. "And Jesus returned in the power of the Spirit into Galilee: and there went out a fame of him through all the region round about" (Luke 4:14). Jesus returned from where? Jesus returned from the wilderness, being alone with God for forty days. Jesus spent time in prayer and fasting until He received God's power. Be led by the Holy Ghost when seeking God for the miraculous. Don't forget, at the beginning of Luke chapter four, the Scripture says, "And Jesus being full of the Holy Ghost returned from Jordan, and was led by the Spirit into the wilderness..." You cannot tap into God's power on your own.

You must be led by the Holy Ghost. The Holy Ghost is the key to the supernatural. He enables us to fast until we get God's answer that we desire. Now we can better understand God's anointing on Jesus and how He obtained it. In Luke chapter four, Jesus said,

> The Spirit of the Lord is upon me, because he hath anointed me to preach the gospel to the poor; he hath sent me to heal the brokenhearted, to preach deliverance to the captives, and recovering of sight to the blind, to set at liberty them that are bruised... And he closed the book, and he gave it again to the minister, and sat down. And the eyes of all them that were in the synagogue were fastened on him. And he began to say unto them, this day is this scripture fulfilled in your ears (Luke 4:18, 20, 21).

The anointing came on Jesus because He willfully paid the price for it.

I ask you, how hungry are you for God's power? Are you willing to do exactly what Jesus did to walk in His awesome power? God deals with every individual differently. But God will require you to pay a price before He can trust you with the Holy Ghost's power. The Scripture says,

> But ye shall receive power, after that the Holy Ghost is come upon you: and ye shall be witnesses unto me both in Jerusalem, and in all Judaea, and in Samaria, and unto the uttermost part of the earth (Acts 1:8).

The Word did not say you will receive power immediately, but "…AFTER the Holy Ghost is come upon you…" After you meet God's requirement for your life, the miracle-working power will come.

Fasting is not a popular topic in the church today. It will never be popular because fasting deals with self-denial.

> …If any man come to me, and hate not his father, and mother, and wife, and children, and brethren, and sisters, yea, and his own life also, he cannot be my disciple. And whosoever doth not bear his cross. and come after me. cannot be my disciple (Luke 14:26-27).

How God Called Me into the Miraculous

In 1999, a very close friend to me and my wife had a reoccurrence of cancer. She and her husband loved us dearly. God's love working through their lives had deeply touched us. I was genuinely concerned and my heart carried a burden to see her totally healed of cancer. I began to seek God.

The desire increased to the point that I searched God's Word on all the healing Scriptures. The Holy Ghost taught me many Scriptures to let me know that healing is God's will for His children. These are some of the many Scriptures:

- I am the LORD that healeth thee (Ex. 15:26).

- Bless the LORD, O my soul: and all that is within me, bless his holy name. Bless the LORD, O my soul, and forget not all his benefits: who forgiveth all thine iniquities; who healeth all thy diseases (Ps. 103:1-3).

- He sent his word, and healed them, and delivered them from their destructions (Ps. 107:20).

- And Jesus went about all Galilee, teaching in their synagogues, and preaching the gospel of the kingdom, and healing all manner of sickness and all manner of disease among the people (Matt. 4:23).

- I say unto you, If ye have faith as a grain of mustard seed, ye shall say unto this mountain, Remove hence to yonder place; and it shall remove; and nothing shall be impossible unto you. Howbeit this kind goeth not out but by prayer and fasting (Matt. 17:20-21).

- How God anointed Jesus of Nazareth with the Holy Ghost and with power: who went about doing good, and healing all that were oppressed of the devil; for God was with him (Acts 10:38).

I had realized that God's Word clearly stated that healing is for His people. I realized that God's healing power was available, but that a price had to be paid. God knocked at my heart's door. I could not deny that, if I was going to tap into God's power to see our friend healed, I had to fast. When God shined the light of this revelation into my heart, I thought God must be kidding if He expected me to fast forty days. But my desire to see healing come to someone in need was far greater than my appetite for food.

I wrestled with God almost half the night. I could not shake the truth He had revealed to my heart. The Holy Ghost also showed me from Scripture that God required the same thing from His apostles. "And, behold, I send the promise of my Father upon you: but tarry ye in the city of Jerusalem, until ye be endued with power from on high" (Luke 24:49). After Jesus had been resurrected from the dead, He commanded His followers to tarry until they received God's miracle power. Jesus knew that, if they were to have the same success in ministry, they had to pay a price.

The apostles obeyed Jesus' command.

> And when the day of Pentecost was fully come, they were all with one accord in one place. And suddenly there came a sound from heaven as of a rushing mighty wind, and it filled all the house where they were sitting. And there appeared unto them cloven tongues like as of fire, and it sat upon each of them. And they were all filled with the Holy Ghost, and began to speak with other tongues, as the Spirit gave them utterance (Acts 2:1-4).

The apostles were alone with God for ten days, seeking Him through fasting and prayer. After they had met God's requirement, the fire fell. The Holy Ghost's fire always falls after much prayer and fasting.

How do we know that the apostles received the power of the Holy Ghost? The Scriptures say, "And with great power gave the apostles witness of the resurrection of the Lord Jesus: and great grace was upon them all" (Acts 4:33). "And by the hands of the apostles were many signs and wonders wrought among the people..." (Acts 5:12).

> ...They brought forth the sick into the streets, and laid them on beds and couches, that at the least the shadow of Peter passing by might overshadow some of them. There came also a multitude out of the cities round about unto Jerusalem, bringing sick folks, and them which were vexed with unclean spirits: and they were healed every one (Acts 5:15-16).

Jesus said these words to His apostles:

> But when the Comforter is come, whom I will send unto you from the Father, even the Spirit of truth, which proceedeth from the Father, he shall testify of me: And ye

also shall bear witness, because ye have been with me from the beginning (John 15:26-27).

The Holy Ghost's power comes to bear witness to the Lord's resurrection. After the apostles received God's miracle-working power, their ministry succeeded in the same manner as Christ's ministry. The blind received sight, the cripples walked, and the dead rose to life.

After much tugging on my heart, I accepted God's call by faith. My call to the miraculous came through a woman suffering from cancer. God's Word is absolutely true in saying, "all things work together for good to them that love God, to them who are the called according to his purpose" (Rom. 8:28). I got my wife's permission to fast for forty days and nights.

On day twenty-one of this fast, our friend died of cancer and went home to be with the Lord. I asked God, "Should I quit fasting?" He replied, "Continue, I have a greater purpose for this fast." My wife and I were shattered, but God encouraged me to continue by comforting our hearts. I don't care who you are, you don't always understand what God is doing in your life. I fasted from October 16 to November 25 of 1999, forty days and forty nights. During my time of fasting, all of hell came against me. The devil tempted me beyond measure to quit fasting, but by God's grace, He saw me through. The Bible says, "I can do all things through Christ which strengtheneth me" (Phil. 4:13).

Two weeks after the fast was over, I was asked by the pastor of our church we were attending to preach an evangelistic service. As I preached that night, God's power suddenly covered me like a blanket of electricity from my head down to my toes. The promised power had finally come. That night, the altar was packed and many people lay around the altar weeping. The first miracle that took place was when I prayed for a woman who was scheduled to have back surgery and she was completely healed by God's power. Since then, my wife and I have seen many marvelous healing miracles, which I will talk about in the next chapter.

A call to the miraculous is going out from God's heart. Will you humbly respond and say yes to God? God looks for anyone who will yield and make themselves available to Him. Jesus said, "...He that believeth on me, the works that I do shall he do also..." Did you get that? Jesus didn't say you had to be an apostle, prophet, evangelist, pastor, or teacher. He said, "He that believeth." Anyone willing to put their faith in Christ and to pay the price, God will empower to perform the supernatural. Jesus made this clear when He said, "...these signs shall follow them that believeth..." The proof of faith is works. According to Jesus, real faith should be an outward manifestation of the miraculous.

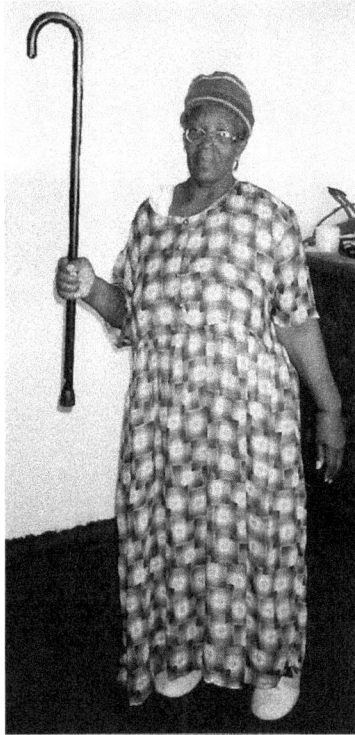

**This lady in Freeport, Grand Bahama suffered a
stroke that left her paralyzed and numb on her
entire left side. Evangelist Sean prayed
the prayer of faith and she was totally healed.**

Evangelist Sean Pinder

Chapter 7
The Impact of the Gospel Followed by Signs, Wonders and Miracles

In this chapter, God's Word brings to light the impact of the Gospel preached with power and demonstration. First, we see this impact in Christ's life, and then we will see it in His followers' lives. Jesus began His ministry preaching in the synagogues. After the people saw the miracles, His ministry increased.

> And Jesus went about all Galilee, teaching in their synagogues, and preaching the gospel of the kingdom, and healing all manner of sickness and all manner of disease among the people. And his fame went throughout all Syria: and they brought unto him all sick people that were taken with divers diseases and torments, and those which were possessed with devils, and those which were lunatick, and those that had the palsy; and he healed them. And there followed him great multitudes of people from Galilee,

65

and from Decapolis, and from Jerusalem,
and from Judaea, and from beyond Jordan
(Matt. 4:23-25).

Further into God's Word, the number of the people
continues to progress. "In the mean time, when there
were gathered together an innumerable multitude of
people, insomuch that they trode one upon another…"
(Luke 12:1).

What drew the people? The answer is obvious.
They came because the Gospel being preached was
followed by an outpouring of miracles. Jesus'
crusades were not dead, but rather alive with God's
power. Insomuch that "…the multitude wondered,
when they saw the dumb to speak, the maimed to be
whole, the lame to walk, and the blind to see: and
they glorified the God of Israel" (Matt. 15:31). God's
power operating compels the people to come. The
Bible declares, "Thy people shall be willing in the day
of thy power…" (Ps. 110:3). God's miracle-working
power in action draws people together in a way that
preaching without miracles would never accomplish.
Jesus went from preaching in the synagogues, to great
multitudes, then to an innumerable multitude of
people.

The same principle Jesus used worked for the
apostles. On the day of Pentecost, Peter had just been
endued with the Holy Ghost's power and had
preached. The results were phenomenal. "Then they

that gladly received his word were baptized: and the same day there were added unto them about three thousand souls" (Acts 2:41). The crowd's growth directly resulted from notable miracles performed in their midst. "...Many of them which heard the word believed; and the number of the men was about five thousand" (Acts 4:4). Increasing miracles brought about an even greater outcome. The apostles witnessed the crowds' growth.

> And by the hands of the apostles were many signs and wonders wrought among the people; (and they were all with one accord in Solomon's porch. And of the rest durst no man join himself to them: but the people magnified them. And believers were the more added to the Lord, multitudes both of men and women.) Insomuch that they brought forth the sick into the streets, and laid them on beds and couches, that at the least the shadow of Peter passing by might overshadow some of them. There came also a multitude out of the cities round about unto Jerusalem, bringing sick folks, and them which were vexed with unclean spirits: and they were healed every one" (Acts 5:12-16).

I love God revealing His Word to us as we are willing to open our hearts to Him. The Gospel, accompanied with God's power, impacts people.

> Then Philip went down to the city of Samaria, and preached Christ unto them. And the people with one accord gave heed unto those things which Philip spake, hearing and seeing the miracles which he did. For unclean spirits, crying with loud voice, came out of many that were possessed with them: and many taken with palsies, and that were lame, were healed. And there was great joy in that city. Now when the apostles which were at Jerusalem heard that Samaria had received the word of God, they sent unto them Peter and John... (Acts 8:5-8, 14).

Jesus is the answer for the nations of the earth. In proclaiming this truth, we must demonstrate the Gospel followed by miracles.

> And it came to pass, as Peter passed throughout all quarters, he came down also to the saints which dwelt at Lydda. And there he found a certain man named Aeneas, which had kept his bed eight years, and was sick of the palsy. And

Peter said unto him, Aeneas, Jesus Christ maketh thee whole: arise, and make thy bed. And he arose immediately. And all that dwelt at Lydda and Saron saw him, and turned to the Lord (Acts 9:32-35).

Two cities gave their lives to Jesus as a result of God performing a miracle of healing on one man.

The book of Acts is a model of God's will for the Church. The sooner we get back to this pattern, the better.

Now there was at Joppa a certain disciple named Tabitha, which by interpretation is called Dorcas: this woman was full of good works and almsdeeds which she did. And it came to pass in those days, that she was sick, and died: whom when they had washed, they laid her in an upper chamber. And forasmuch as Lydda was nigh to Joppa, and the disciples had heard that Peter was there, they sent unto him two men, desiring him that he would not delay to come to them. Then Peter arose and went with them. When he was come, they brought him into the upper chamber: and all the widows stood by him weeping and shewing the coats and garments which Dorcas made, while she was with them. But Peter put them all forth, and kneeled down, and prayed; and turning him to the body said, Tabitha, arise. And she opened her eyes: and when she saw Peter, she sat up. And he gave her his hand, and lifted her up, and when he had called the saints and widows, presented her alive. And it was known throughout all Joppa; and many believed in the Lord (Acts 9:36-42).

Sinners are drawn to Jesus whenever they see proof that He is alive. Many believed in the Lord because a notable miracle had been performed.

And God wrought special miracles by the hands of Paul: So that from his body were brought unto the sick handkerchiefs or aprons, and the diseases departed from them, and the evil spirits went out of them. And many that believed came, and confessed, and shewed their deeds. Many of them also which used curious arts brought their books together, and burned them before all men: and they counted the price of them, and found it fifty thousand pieces of silver. So mightily grew the word of God and prevailed (Acts 19:11-12, 18, 19).

God's word prevailed. "…God wrought special miracles by the hands of Paul…"

God's power worked so mightily through the apostles that their ministries increased. First, we see three thousand saved; the numbers then increased to five thousand, then multitudes, and then the Bible says the entire city of Samaria received God's Word. But it doesn't stop. It gets even better. The enemies of this radical group of apostles feared, saying, "…These that have turned the world upside down are come hither also…" (Acts 17:6). The demonstration of the Gospel can have such an impact that even our worst enemies will be forced to confess that we are world-shakers.

In the apostles' day, the known world felt the impact of the Gospel. I believe with all my heart the day is here when we will touch this entire world by demonstrating God's power. I remember in the Uganda, Africa crusade, we learned that the witch doctors were sending messages to each other about the crusade, saying, "Too much power." They knew that they were no match for the Gospel followed by a demonstration of Holy Ghost power. Jesus Himself said, "Behold, I give unto you power to tread on serpents and scorpions, and over all the power of the enemy: and nothing shall by any means hurt you" (Luke 10:19).

This little baby's arm was broken when he came to the crusade. Here, Evangelist Aimee demonstrates that the baby's arm has been healed, totally restored by God's power.

Chapter 8
Why are Miracles Lightly Esteemed?

After my wife and I tapped into God's power, much opposition arose against us. Some preachers stood in their pulpits, quoting the famous verse used against ministers with miracle ministries,

> Many will say to me in that day, Lord, Lord, have we not prophesied in thy name? And in thy name have cast out devils? And in thy name done many wonderful works? And then will I profess unto them, I never knew you: depart from me, ye that work iniquity (Matt. 7:22-23).

The improper use of this Scripture haunted us, so we earnestly sought an answer from God. Judas, one of Jesus' disciples, was used mightily in the miracle ministry, yet he betrayed the Lord. Jesus Himself revealed that Judas did not make it into heaven when He said, "…Woe unto that man by whom the Son of man is betrayed! It had been good for that man if he had not been born" (Matt. 26:24).

We were deeply troubled by the words "…Then will I profess unto them, I never knew you: depart from me, ye that work iniquity..." I thought, "Lord, if they have done so many mighty works in your name, how can you say, '…I never knew you…'?" I am confident that those walking in God's power have been wrongfully attacked with these Scriptures. One night, as I read the book of Ezekiel, God answered our heart's cry. God's light broke into our hearts when I read this verse.

> When I shall say to the righteous, that he shall surely live; if he trust to his own righteousness, and commit iniquity, all his righteousnesses shall not be remembered; but for his iniquity that he hath committed, he shall die for it (Eze. 33:13).

Do you see the connection? If someone used in the miracle ministry backslides and turns his back on God, "…all his righteousnesses shall not be remembered..." This is the reason Jesus will answer "…I never knew you: depart from me, ye that work iniquity…"

Jesus said, "Many will say to me in that day…" He did not say all, but He did say many. My heart found much comfort knowing that you can have the power of God and stay faithful to Him just as Paul and the other apostles did. Some love to use the Scriptures to discredit the miracle ministry and cause others to doubt genuine men of God.

There are two sides to every coin. On the one hand, we see Jesus warning those who walk in God's power to stay faithful to Him. On the other hand, we see Jesus giving a stern warning to those who would oppose real men of God with miracle ministries. "And John answered and said, Master, we saw one casting out devils in thy name; and we forbad him, because he followeth not with us. And Jesus said unto him, Forbid him not: for he that is not against us is for us" (Luke 9:49-50). Jesus was talking to his disciples and said, "Forbid him not." The word "forbid" means "to hinder; keep from; withstand."[8] Some have tried to hinder us, but have failed miserably in their attempts. Some have resisted us and shut doors to discourage us from the call of God. But, like the apostle Paul, we "...Press toward the mark for the prize of the high calling of God in Christ Jesus" (Phil. 3:14).

Realize that everyone is not going to rejoice for you when you tap into God's miracle-working power. When God's power manifests in your life, you will begin to see by God's Spirit who your real friends are. Peter, James, and John were fine with the religious leaders as long as they were fishermen. But as soon

---

8 Ibid

as God's power came into their lives, they became a threat to the Pharisees, who wanted the apostles dead. The apostle Paul experienced this same persecution and wrote,

> Now as Jannes and Jambres withstood Moses, so do these also resist the truth: men of corrupt minds, reprobate concerning the faith. But they shall proceed no further: for their folly shall be manifest unto all men, as theirs also was (2 Tim. 3:8-9).

Paul warns us that people will take miracle ministries lightly because their minds are corrupt. Moses had one of the most powerful miracle ministries in the Bible, yet he was resisted. When Moses stood before Pharaoh and threw down his rod, his enemies resisted and copied his miracle. In the end, God's power prevailed.

> And Moses and Aaron went in unto Pharaoh, and they did so as the LORD had commanded: and Aaron cast down his rod before Pharaoh, and before his servants, and it became a serpent. Then Pharaoh also called the wise men and the sorcerers: now the magicians of Egypt, they also did in like manner with their enchantments. For they cast down every

man his rod, and they became serpents: but Aaron's rod swallowed up their rods (Ex. 7:10-12).

Jesus shared much light concerning the miraculous when He said, "But if I with the finger of God cast out devils, no doubt the kingdom of God is come upon you" (Luke 11:20). The miracle ministry is taken lightly. Many do not realize that miracles are the finger of God and the manifestation of the kingdom of God. Other Scriptures reveal much truth along these lines. Jesus strongly stated,

If thou hadst known, even thou, at least in this thy day, the things which belong unto thy peace! but now they are hid from thine eyes. For the days shall come upon thee, that thine enemies shall cast a trench about thee, and compass thee round, and keep thee in on every side, and shall lay thee even with the ground, and thy children within thee; and they shall not leave in thee one stone upon another; because thou knewest not the time of thy visitation (Luke 19:42-44).

The miracle ministry is lightly esteemed because many do not recognize signs, wonders and miracles as a visitation from God. Jesus could make this statement because no one else in the entire Bible performed as many miracles as Jesus did. He repeatedly told the people "…The works which the Father hath given me to finish, the same works that I do, bear witness of me, that the Father hath sent me" (John 5:36). The miracles Jesus performed bore witness to the truth He preached. No one could deny that God was with Him.

The miracle ministry is also lightly esteemed for other reasons. Another reason is that some do not identify the seriousness and the responsibility that comes along with seeing God's power demonstrated. Christ strongly rebuked the cities that experienced God's power.

> Then began he to upbraid the cities wherein most of his mighty works were done, because they repented not: Woe unto thee, Chorazin! Woe unto thee, Bethsaida! for if the mighty works, which were done in you, had been done in Tyre and Sidon, they would have repented long ago in sackcloth and ashes. But I say unto you, It shall be more tolerable for Tyre and Sidon at the day of judgment, than for you. And thou, Capernaum, which art exalted unto heaven, shalt be brought down to hell: for if the mighty works, which have been done in thee, had

been done in Sodom, it would have remained until this day. But I say unto you, That it shall be more tolerable for the land of Sodom in the day of judgment, than for thee" (Matt. 11:20-24).

The town demoniac, Muyingo, was set free after Evangelist Sean prayed during this miracle crusade.

When Muyingo's mother saw how God delivered her son, she gave her own heart to Jesus that same night.

No one seemed to notice the rain as the whole crowd went crazy, rejoicing over what God had done.

A brand new Muyingo, who is now properly clothed and in his right mind.

Evangelist Sean gave the new believer clothes, for which Muyingo was clearly grateful.

This little Bahamian girl was healed of the lumps in her groin by God's mighty power.

Evangelists Sean and Aimee Pinder are a dynamic husband-and-wife team.

Together, they are shaking and impacting lives with the uncompromising Gospel and the miracle-working power of Jesus Christ.

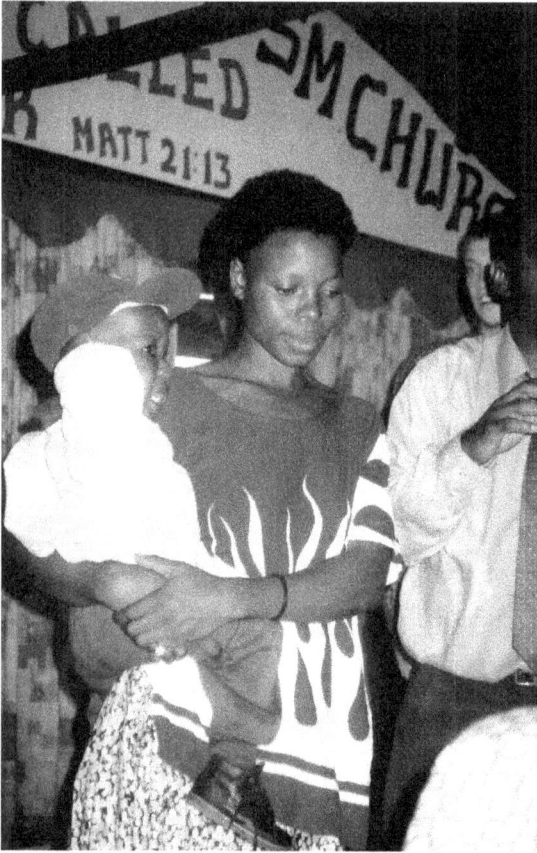

For five years, every time this woman had a
bowel movement, she had to push her
intestines back in. While Evangelist Aimee
rebuked sickness, this woman was completely
healed of her condition.

Part Two

Accounts of the Miraculous

This lady had arthritis so bad, she couldn't climb stairs. After this service, she ran up and down stairs with ease at the New Orleans meeting.

This woman had crippling pain in her feet and couldn't walk without support. She was in her house when she heard Evangelist Sean preaching during a Pastors' Conference. She walked to that night's Crusade, healed and completely pain-free.

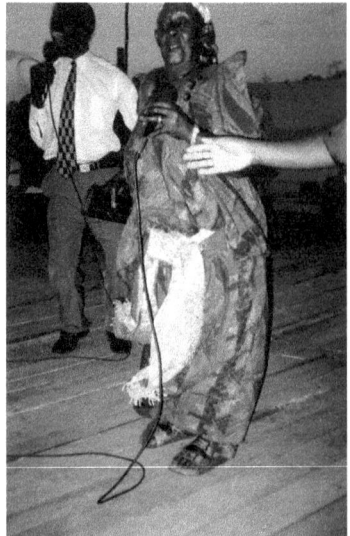

Chapter 9
Lonoke, Arkansas

And they went forth, and preached everywhere, the Lord working with them, and confirming the word with signs following. Amen (Mark 16:20).

Tonight, the service was awesome. A strong outbreak of praises to God happened. Many paced back and forth, weeping before the Lord. God's miracle-working power was ready to perform the miraculous. The Holy Ghost spoke to my heart, letting me know it's time to minister to the sick. I made an altar call for those who needed a miracle of healing in their bodies to come forward in faith.

Many responded with great expectation "and the power of the Lord was present to heal them" (Luke 5:17).

Woman Blind in Right Eye Receives Sight

One of the great miracles that stood out to me was an old woman, strong in faith, who was completely blind in her right eye. I laid hands on her right eye in Jesus' mighty Name, and when I removed my hand, she shouted, "I can see, I can see!" The crowd burst out into praises to God.

Indeed, a notable miracle had been done. God gave that loving woman 20/20 eyesight. Glory to God!

> ...The multitude wondered, when they saw the dumb to speak, the maimed to be whole, the lame to walk, and the blind to see: and they glorified the God of Israel (Matt. 15:31).

Truck Driver's Knee Cap Recreated

In the miracle services during this week, another outstanding miracle occurred. A six-foot truck driver's knee cap had been surgically removed. He was unable to walk without the aid of his cane. He believed God could heal him. Aimee and I laid hands on that leg in Jesus' Name and prayed the prayer of faith. As we did, God's power began to work. We could feel something moving underneath our hands. God recreated the man's knee cap right in our midst. That tender-hearted gentleman raised his cane in the air and began to walk back and forth on the stage. He did not even limp as he demonstrated he had been completely healed by God's miracle-working power. Much praises went up to God. God's presence saturated the atmosphere. He wept as he glorified

God. "…The prayer of faith shall save the sick, and the Lord shall raise him up" (James 5:15).

Sixty-Five-Year-Old Woman Receives Perfect Hearing

Electricity filled the atmosphere. A sixty-five-year-old woman was born with a hole in one eardrum, causing that ear to have about ten percent hearing. Instantly, she received perfect hearing. She testified that she knew the hole in her ear drum was completely closed by God's power. She could now hear a whisper perfectly out of that ear. Her husband was very grateful to God. The people were amazed. "He hath done all things well: he maketh both the deaf to hear, and the dumb to speak" (Mark 7:37).

Young Woman's Deaf Ear Opened

Another miracle took place in Lonoke. God's miracle anointing manifested through awesome demonstrations. In this particular service, a woman who had been completely deaf in one ear came for prayer. I placed my finger in her ear and commanded her ear to open. It did. After prayer, she heard perfectly out of that ear. She wept, knowing God had compassion on her. She testified, saying, "I felt warm oil going into my ear."

And they bring unto him one that was deaf, and had an impediment in his speech; and they beseech him to put his hand upon him. And he took him aside from the multitude, and put his fingers into his ears, and he spit, and touched his tongue; And looking up to heaven, he sighed, and saith unto him, Ephphatha, that is, Be opened. And straightway his ears were opened... (Mark 7:32-35).

Woman's Lump in Breast Vanished

Whenever God's power is displayed, things begin to happen that increase our faith and trust in Him. A woman who had a lump in her breast came expecting God to heal her. After the prayer of faith, we told her to go to the ladies' restroom to check if the lump had vanished. She came back in amazement and much excitement, saying, "The lump is gone. I cannot find it." Prior to this miracle service, the doctor had examined her. They wanted to run more tests on the lump to find out if it was cancerous. Her appointment was scheduled to return for tests the day after God had healed her. I told her, "When you go back, the doctor will be confounded." The next night, this woman testified that she went back to the doctor and they were confused. They could not find the lump. The church shouted, giving God all the glory for the marvelous things He had done. "O LORD my God, I cried unto thee, and thou hast healed me" (Psalms 30:2).

Thirty-Five-Year-Old Woman Receives Jesus

Miracles are great. We must never forget their purpose. Miracles bring people into a reality that Jesus is alive and not dead. In the midst of all these strong demonstrations, something took place that I will never forget. A woman walked up to the altar, weeping. I said, "Madam, what do you want the Lord to do for you?" She said, "I want to give my heart to Jesus." My heart melted. The love of God can be overwhelming. It was not good preaching that drew this woman to the altar. She saw with her own two eyes that Jesus was alive and still at work. After she repeated the prayer of salvation, her countenance shined.

> And he said unto her, Thy sins are forgiven. And they that sat at meat with him began to say within themselves, who is this that forgiveth sins also? And he said to the woman, Thy faith hath saved thee; go in peace (Luke 7:48-50).

Twelve-Year-Old Boy Gives His Life to Jesus

There is nothing on the face of this planet as precious as the Holy Ghost's anointing. I am madly in love with Jesus. Jesus is truly my all in all. We are nothing apart from Him. God's power flowed wonderfully. God's sweet presence filled the entire place. Suddenly, I saw a woman come to the altar with a young boy. I asked the mother what was her son's request. She replied, "My son wants to give his life to Jesus." He was so touched by all the miracles that they drew him to the foot of the Cross. I led him in a simple prayer and he was gloriously saved. I love God's power in action, but there is nothing as dear to God's heart as a lost soul. "…If thou shalt confess with thy mouth the Lord Jesus, and shalt believe in thine heart that God hath raised him from the dead, thou shalt be saved" (Rom. 10:9).

Chapter 10
Little Rock, Arkansas

And when he had called unto him his twelve disciples, he gave them power against unclean spirits, to cast them out, and to heal all manner of sickness and all manner of disease (Matt. 10:1).

Forty-Eight-Year-Old Man's Heart Recreated

My wife and I knew a man who had suffered from severe chest pains on a Friday afternoon. His wife encouraged him to go to the hospital. An MRI showed the doctors that his arteries had a blockage. Doctors discussed possible methods to remove the blockage through either an angioplasty or open-heart surgery. On Sunday afternoon, the Holy Ghost said to me, "Go and pray for this gentleman and I will heal him." I obeyed and went to the hospital to visit with him. We talked and I shared many of the healing Scriptures. Suddenly, God's presence came into that room. The man looked at me and said, "Pray for me. I am ready." I laid hands on his chest in Jesus' Name. As I did, he said, "I felt a warm pressure go across my chest and I know God just healed me." I said,

"Tomorrow, when they check you, please give me a call." I could not wait to get that phone call.

Monday finally came when he was scheduled for an arteriogram. The gentleman gave me a call from the hospital with great excitement, saying, "The doctors did one final test. The doctor turned to the nurse and said, 'This guy has arteries and a heart of a twenty-year-old man. There is no blockage here. Nothing is wrong. No surgery. [Turning to the patient, our friend, the doctor said,] I will give you a clean bill of health.'" To God belongs all the glory, honor and praise. "…With God all things are possible" (Matt. 19:26).

Nine-Year-Old Girl's Hearing Restored

I preached a healing service in Little Rock, Arkansas. God's presence was awesome. A little girl with precious child-like faith came forward for prayer, believing God to heal her ears. She had failed a hearing test performed by a nurse at an elementary school. The test proved that she had lost sixty percent of her hearing in both ears. I stuck my finger in both of her ears in Jesus' Name and asked God to heal her ears.

She was scheduled to go to the doctor the next week at the local children's hospital for some tests to be done. After the tests were performed, the results showed that the young girl had passed the hearing tests. Her ears were normal. She later testified that, when she received prayer, her ears popped. What an awesome God we serve. Later in the week, we communicated with the young girl. She was full of joy. She heard every word perfectly. Praise God! "Therefore I say unto you, what things soever ye desire, when ye pray, believe that ye receive them, and ye shall have them" (Mark 11:24).

Young Man's Torn Tendons Healed

In a service that we conducted, a young man that I knew well came in on crutches. He told us that, earlier that day, while playing a game of basketball, he tore some ligaments in his foot and was taken to the hospital. The doctor told him that it would take six to eight weeks to heal and gave him a pair of crutches. He could not walk without them.

In that service, God's power manifested. The Holy Ghost prompted me to go and pray for him. As I did, his leg began to shake under the power of God. The swelling begin to go down. After laying hands on that leg the fifth time, he got up and walked without his crutches. Even though God had just miraculously healed him, he still had a slight limp. By the next day, he was walking perfectly. What should have taken six to eight weeks, God did in a matter of about twenty-four hours. Jesus had proven again that He is still "the same yesterday, and today, and forever" (Heb. 13:8).

Young Woman with Cracked Vertebrae Healed

In another healing service, a young woman suffered from a cracked vertebra. During prayer for the sick, she came forward, believing God. She was scheduled for surgery. We laid hands on her in the Name of Jesus. After the prayer of faith, she was completely healed and free from all of her intense pain. God supernaturally joined the cracked vertebrae back together and made them whole. Praise God the surgery was cancelled. "Behold, I am the LORD, the God of all flesh: is there anything too hard for me?" (Jer. 32:27).

Woman with Three Ruptured Discs Healed

Miracles approve the preaching of Jesus Christ. A woman who worked at a heavy machinery company was required to do heavy lifting. As a result, she had ruptured three discs in her lower back. For a long time, she suffered from her condition. Medications gave her little relief. She came forward, believing God for a miracle. After the laying on of hands, she began to weep and praise God. She bent down and touched her toes a few times, demonstrating she had been completely healed. "...all things, whatsoever ye shall ask in prayer, believing, ye shall receive" (Matt. 21:22).

Woman Healed of Dyslexia

A woman who had dyslexia for twenty-six years came to one of our services. When she read, her condition caused her to see blank pages instead of words. God's anointing moved in a powerful way. She came believing God to heal her from her learning disorder. After dyslexia was rebuked in the Name of Jesus, we handed her a Bible to read. She read an entire chapter out loud with no problems. Three days later, she read an entire book for the first time in her life. Before her healing, she had only read books halfway through and never in their entirety. She was happy to finally be able to finish a book with no difficulties. "...Himself took our infirmities, and bare our sicknesses" (Matt. 8:17).

Boy With Broken Arm Healed

I preached a service where God moved powerfully. In this service, a boy about the age of thirteen believed God to heal his broken arm that was in a cast. After he had received prayer, he was healed instantly. We had him exercise the hand to demonstrate that he had been healed. To everyone's amazement, he moved his hand up and down perfectly and did things that are impossible for someone with a broken hand to do. Everyone's faith was elevated as a result of that miracle. They began to praise God.

> But without faith it is impossible to please him: for he that cometh to God must believe that he is, and that he is a rewarder of them that diligently seek him (Heb. 11:6).

Man Comes Out of a Coma

I got a phone call one day that a young man on a motorcycle had a head-on collision with another vehicle. This young man was rushed to the hospital, being in a coma. He was expected to be in this condition for a long time. His mother was told by the doctors that he would have a 50/50 chance of coming out of his coma.

I got to the hospital and the faith of God stirred deep in my soul. I spoke with his mother, comforting her with words from the Holy Ghost that all was going to be well. I went and prayed for this man in the hospital room. I felt God's presence really strong. After the prayer of faith, I left and went home, convinced in my spirit that God had begun working a miracle of healing on his body. I got a phone call later that day. Exactly two hours after I had left, that young man came out of the coma. Praise God! The next day, he was released from the hospital. God never fails to amaze me over and over again. "If thou canst believe, all things are possible to him that believeth" (Mark 9:23).

The crowd listens eagerly as Evangelist Sean Pinder brings the message of the Gospel to Uganda, Africa in the Miracle Crusade.

Evangelist Sean Pinder

Chapter 11
Mabelvale, Arkansas

He sent his word, and healed them, and delivered them from their destructions (Psalms 107:20).

Woman Healed from Degenerative Disc in Her Lower Back

In the miracle services held in Mabelvale, the healing anointing was present to heal God's people. A woman came for prayer, believing to be healed from a degenerative disc in her lower back. As Aimee and I laid hands on her, we felt God's power at work. We had her demonstrate that she had been healed. She bent all the way down and touched her toes a few times. She twisted her body from side to side. Then she ran back and forth a few times. All the pain had left her back and she was completely healed. When we put our trust in God, He performs the impossible.

Healed from Blood Clots in the Leg

In the same service, a pastor came forward in faith, believing that God was going to heal him. He suffered from blood clots in his legs. This caused him intense pain. We laid hands on him and God began to work on his behalf. After the prayer of faith, all the pain in his leg had disappeared. He began to run back and forth to demonstrate that he was totally pain free. "And they cast out many devils, and anointed with oil many that were sick, and healed them" (Mark 6:13).

Chapter 12
Benton, Arkansas

And Jesus went about all the cities and villages, teaching in their synagogues, and preaching the gospel of the kingdom, and healing every sickness and every disease among the people (Matt. 9:35).

Man Healed Who Fell Twelve Feet

In the church that I pastored in Benton, a member came to church on a Sunday morning with a cane. He shared how, while he was working, he accidentally slipped and fell from twelve feet. His nail gun also fell and shot a nail into his knee. He was in intense pain and in bad shape. During the worship, God's power came to perform the miraculous. The man came in faith, believing to be healed.

As I laid hands on him, I felt God's power going into his body. I knew something great was about to happen. God had me take his cane from him. This man got so touched and infused by the healing anointing, that he began to run and jump, demonstrating that he was perfectly healed. We shouted, screamed, and praised God for performing

105

such a miracle. "…All the people rejoiced for all the glorious things that were done by him" (Luke 13:17).

Fractured Leg Healed

A young woman who attended our church was in a car accident that fractured her leg. She believed that God was going to heal her. After the prayer of faith, all the pain left and she was completely healed. She stood and walked back and forth to demonstrate her healing.

Stomach Ulcers Healed

A young lady who suffered from intense stomach ulcers came to church, believing God to heal her stomach. After the prayer of faith, she was completely healed and free from all of her stomach ulcers. To demonstrate that she had been healed, that evening, when she went home, she drank juice that would normally have caused her much pain. Nothing happened. It didn't hurt anymore. She never had any stomach problems again. "Daughter, thy faith hath made thee whole; go in peace, and be whole of thy plague" (Mark 5:34).

Chapter 13
Freeport, Bahamas

For verily I say unto you, That whosoever shall say unto this mountain, Be thou removed, and be thou cast into the sea; and shall not doubt in his heart, but shall believe that those things which he saith shall come to pass; he shall have whatsoever he saith (Mark 11:23).

Man with Broken Leg Healed

I remember preaching a miracle service in the city of Freeport. God's presence swept through the church very powerfully. A man had suffered from a broken leg eight days prior to that miracle service. He was wearing his cast and, obviously, he was unable to walk without his crutches. The Holy Ghost said, "Pray for him and I will heal him tonight."

The atmosphere charged with the healing anointing. I laid hands on his broken leg and, being led by the Holy Ghost, I said, "Walk." I took his crutches. He began to walk and then run without his crutches. When the people saw that miracle of healing, they began to scream, run, jump, fall out under the power, and praise God without restraint.

The only thing people didn't do that night was walk on their hands and stand on their heads!

The people's faith touched God. My friend, in this type of atmosphere, anything can happen. The man demonstrated that God had made him perfectly whole.

> Then Peter said, Silver and gold have I none; but such as I have give I thee: In the name of Jesus Christ of Nazareth rise up and walk. And he took him by the right hand, and lifted him up: and immediately his feet and ankle bones received strength. And he leaping up stood, and walked, and entered with them into the temple, walking, and leaping, and praising God. And all the people saw him walking and praising God... (Acts 3:6-9).

Paralyzed Woman Healed

In the service just mentioned, a woman present was paralyzed from a stroke. She was unable to work. The anointing manifested so strong that you knew God would work on her behalf. As I laid hands on her, I felt God's healing power go into her body. I said to her, "Your healing will manifest any day." There was no physical evidence that she was healed.

A year later, my wife and I were in a parking lot and we were about to get into our car when we heard someone calling us. We did not recognize the woman, but she knew who we were. She walked to where we were and began to testify, saying, "Two weeks after you laid hands and prayed for me, my body was completely healed." We were amazed at how normal she looked compared to when we saw her last, paralyzed from a stroke. She has returned to her job. "Daughter, thy faith hath made thee whole; go in peace, and be whole of thy plague" (Mark 5:34).

Man Going Blind in Both Eyes Receives Clear Vision

In Freeport at another church, we held a miracle service on a Sunday morning. Preaching was a bit tough, but God had great things in mind for His people. One part in the service, I broke and wept. Suddenly, the Lord's power was there to confirm the preaching of the Gospel with miracles. Prompted by the Holy Ghost, I called for those who needed a miracle of healing in their bodies.

A man in his fifties was going blind from diabetes. He came forward for prayer. After the laying on of hands, I asked him to look around the church. Amazed, he could see perfectly clear. He raised his hands to heaven and walked around the sanctuary, weeping. He demonstrated his healing to the congregation by reading signs that were forty to fifty feet away from him. It was awesome to witness this miracle.

After that miracle, the people's faith went to another level in God. I was touched deeply and stirred in my spirit with God's compassion and love. It's impossible to remain the same when God pours out his love on His people so graciously. "...for I am the LORD that healeth thee" (Ex. 15:26).

Thirty Year Back Pain Healed

We held a miracle service in Hunters, Grand Bahama. God's power exploded. A woman suffered thirty years from back problems due to a car wreck. The doctors had prescribed many different medications for her, but her situation only got worse. Aimee and I laid hands on her in Jesus' Name and commanded her back to be made whole.

After the laying on of hands, she was completely healed. She was free from all the pain. She wept and praised God. She said, "I feel warm oil flowing into my back and it flowed where the pain was. I am completely healed and free from all my pain." She bent up and down, twisting her body from one side to the other, demonstrating her healing. Praise God. "...He was wounded for our transgressions, he was bruised for our iniquities: the chastisement of our peace was upon him; and with his stripes we are healed" (Isa. 53:5).

Little Girl's Mumps Vanished

A little girl who suffered from mumps came to one of our miracle services. Her mother and father brought her for prayer. Prior to the service, they had taken her to the doctor and gotten medication, but the mumps would not go away. Their faith for a miracle was strong. After laying hands on the young child, the swelling vanished instantly by God's power. Her parents were grateful and worshipped God. "…Heal the sick that are therein, and say unto them, the kingdom of God is come nigh unto you" (Luke 10:9).

Twenty Year Pinched Nerve in Back Healed

In one of the miracle services, a man suffering twenty years from a pinched nerve in his back came believing for a miracle from God. Having intense pain in the back area for twenty years is no light thing at all. This man was humble and gentle. As I laid hands on him, I felt God's healing power go into his body. He began to lift both hands and weep. He knew God was at work in his body.

After the prayer of faith, he was instantly healed. He touched his toes and exercised his body, doing things he could not do before. This was a holy moment before God. Nothing compares to God's miracle-working power manifesting before your eyes. "Now when the sun was setting, all they that had any sick with divers diseases brought them unto him; and he laid his hands on every one of them, and healed them" (Luke 4:40).

Elderly Man's Stiff Leg Healed

I remember teaching God's Word on the subject of healing in a miracle service. Faith was strong in the atmosphere for God to manifest His power. A man had a stiff leg. His leg could not bend, causing him to depend on a cane to walk. He came in faith to be healed.

As I prayed for this man, God began to touch his entire body. I knew that he was healed. I took his cane from him and he rose up, healed by God's power. He ran back and forth, testifying that he was unable to run for the past fifteen years of his life. This man wept and asked me to lead him in the prayer of salvation. He received the double cure. His leg was completely healed and his sins were forgiven.

Bless the LORD, O my soul: and all that is within me, bless his holy name. Bless the LORD, O my soul, and forget not all his benefits: Who forgiveth all thine iniquities; who healeth all thy diseases... (Psalms 103:1-3).

Elderly Woman Suffering from Two Strokes Healed

A woman explained to me that her mom had suffered from two strokes and was paralyzed in her right side. She asked me if I could go to her mom's house and pray for her. I agreed, and along with my assistants, we went to the house. Upon arrival, the old woman struggled on a cane to walk. Her right side, from her neck all the way down to her toes, had lost all feeling. This old woman had a lot of faith in God. I laid hands on her body and prayed the prayer of faith for her body to be healed. The healing power went into her body and began to work.

After prayer, there was no physical evidence that God was at work, but I knew power went into her body. As we sat and continued to talk, suddenly the old woman said, "I think I just felt something on my right side." By the Spirit, I said, "I believe God is healing you. Get up and walk." She jumped up, lifted the cane in the air, and walked perfectly. We got excited! It was a miracle of God. We checked her and she could feel through the right side of her body again. The grandkids ran out of the room in amazement that Mama was walking, unaided by her cane. "If ye shall ask any thing in my name, I will do it" (John 14:14).

Evangelist Sean Pinder

Chapter 14
Fort Myers, Florida

God also bearing them witness, both with signs and wonders, and with divers miracles, and gifts of the Holy Ghost, according to his own will (Heb. 2:4).

I love preaching the Gospel of Jesus Christ. Aimee and I conducted a miracle service in Fort Meyers. I had great anticipation and anxiously awaited the moment when God's power would manifest to heal His people. After preaching the Gospel, I called for those who needed a healing miracle in their bodies. Many responded in faith.

Woman with a Metal Rod in Her Back Completely Healed

A woman came forward who had suffered a back injury in a car accident. She went through intense surgery as a rod was placed in her back. She was in this condition for fifteen years. It was scientifically impossible for her to ever be able to bend again and touch her toes. Her genuine, childlike faith touched the heart of God. We laid hands on her and God's power began to work. Suddenly, she could bend over and touch her toes. She twisted her body. Up and down she went, touching her toes to demonstrate she was completely healed. Her sister, who saw what God did, began to weep and praise God. In a moment, the entire service's atmosphere became electrified with faith and God's power. In a service such as this, you pray you never come out of such a rich atmosphere of the Holy Ghost's anointing.

> ...He was teaching in one of the synagogues on the Sabbath. And, behold, there was a woman which had a spirit of infirmity eighteen years, and was bowed together, and could in no wise lift up herself. And when Jesus saw her, he called her to him, and said unto her, Woman, thou art loosed from thine infirmity. And he laid his hands on her: and immediately she was made straight, and glorified God" (Luke 13:10-13).

Man Receives Hearing in Deaf Right Ear

In the same service, I prayed for a man who was completely deaf in his right ear. He had this condition for a long time. After the laying on of hands, his right ear popped open and he could hear perfectly.

At the front of the church, I had him place his finger in his left ear to demonstrate his healing. His back was to his wife, so he could not see her. We had his wife walk to the back of the church and speak in a normal tone of voice. We never told him where we asked his wife to stand. As she spoke, he heard every word perfectly. We then asked him to turn around to see where his wife was standing. He began to weep tenderly and praise God when he realized how far his wife was from where he was standing and how he could now hear. His wife also was thrilled beyond measure because God had healed him. "God anointed Jesus of Nazareth with the Holy Ghost and with power: who went about doing good, and healing all that were oppressed of the devil; for God was with him" (Acts 10:38).

Neck Pains Vanished

A woman in the choir came forward and testified about her healing. She suffered from a neck injury caused by a car accident from five years ago. No medications from the doctors brought her relief. When the power of God fell in that service, she was instantly healed. She moved her head up, down, and all around to demonstrate her miracle of healing. "He sent his word, and healed them, and delivered them from their destructions" (Psalms 107:20).

Eyeglasses No Longer Needed

God's power was very strong to heal the people. Many healings took place that night. God's miracle power had the entire atmosphere charged. About six people came forward to testify that they could see clearly without their eyeglasses. Some read aloud without their eyeglasses, demonstrating that God had given them clear vision. To God belongs all the glory.

Chapter 15
New Orleans, Louisiana

There was a man of the Pharisees, named Nicodemus, a ruler of the Jews: The same came to Jesus by night, and said unto him, Rabbi, we know that thou art a teacher come from God: for no man can do these miracles that thou doest, except God be with him (John 3:1-2).

Man's Back Fused Together at Three Levels in the Spine Healed

In the healing services held in New Orleans, the anointing was mighty as I preached the Word of God. After preaching, I was inspired by the Holy Ghost to rebuke sickness out of people's bodies. I asked everyone to place their hands on the part of their bodies that needed healing. The Holy Ghost's power moved among God's people.

Afterwards, I told people to do things they could not do to demonstrate that God was healing their bodies. Suddenly, a man in his forties began to bend and touch his toes. He ran around the church and the people burst out in praises to God. The entire congregation knew this man and knew that he had received a miracle.

I had the gentleman come up and testify what God did for him. He told me how, a few years ago, he worked at a plant. A heavy metal gate fell on him, pinning him to the ground for about twelve hours until he was rescued. He was rushed to the hospital by an ambulance. The doctors performed emergency surgery on him because his back had been crushed. His back was fused together at three levels in the spine. After surgery, he was on disability. But, in that healing service, as sickness was rebuked, the Holy Ghost touched him and he was completely healed. He demonstrated his healing by bending back and forth, running, and jumping. "…The whole multitude sought to touch him: for there went virtue out of him, and healed them all" (Luke 6:19).

Woman's Right Side Paralyzed from a Stroke Healed

God's power was moving in a tangible way. An elderly woman suffered from a stroke, which caused the right side of her body to have no feelings. She was unable to walk without her walking stick. She jumped up and began to walk without her walking stick. All of the feelings returned into her right side. God's power was so strong that she was walking without the stick and didn't realize that she was completely healed.

When she finally realized what God had done for her, she began to weep. What an awesome outpouring of the miraculous! Many more healings took place in this particular service. Arthritis, diabetes, and cancer were totally healed. Also, about six people received healing in their eyes and did not need reading glasses anymore.

> ...Jesus went about all Galilee, teaching in their synagogues, and preaching the gospel of the kingdom, and healing all manner of sickness and all manner of disease among the people (Matt. 4:23).

Little Girl Healed from Poor Eyesight

God's healing power swept through the entire congregation. A little girl came up to the platform weeping and testified that her eyesight was now clear. She no longer needed her eyeglasses. The girl's mother wept much. There was no denying that God had healed her daughter.

School Teacher Healed of Arthritis

A school teacher had arthritis for a long time. She sat in one of our miracle services. Due to her suffering from arthritis, she could not walk up and down stairs or run. God's power broke through into the sanctuary to the point that faith was extremely strong. God began to heal many while they were worshipping Him. This school teacher was instantly healed and began running, showing everyone in her church that she was now healed. She also went into the foyer and ran up and down the stairs as proof of her healing.

> And when the men of that place had knowledge of him, they sent out into all that country round about, and brought unto him all that were diseased; And besought him that they might only touch the hem of his garment: and as many as touched were made perfectly whole (Matt. 14:35-36).

Chapter 16
Uganda, Africa

*And the LORD will take away from thee all sickness...
(Deut. 7:15).*

The pastors' conference and miracle crusade we held in Uganda was awesome. It is difficult to communicate with words the many miracles that God performed. We had a group of people recording the miracles and they could not keep up because of so many miracles that took place. In this chapter, I will tell you some of the great miracles that God performed. I know if you are in need of a miracle from God, your faith will be strengthened from reading about these awesome miracles.

Boy Born Deaf in Right Ear Healed

The first service I preached in Uganda was greeted by looks of unbelief. I love a good fight! God will vindicate Himself if you trust Him. During the prayer for the sick, a nine-year-old boy, who was born deaf in his right ear, came for prayer, believing that his ear would open. I stuck my finger in his right ear and commanded the spirit of deafness to come out.

In an instant, the boy's ear opened and he could hear perfectly in his right ear. When that first miracle took place, the people came alive. We checked this young boy's ear. He could hear every sound we made perfectly.

> And my speech and my preaching was not with enticing words of man's wisdom, but in demonstration of the Spirit and of power: That your faith should not stand in the wisdom of men, but in the power of God (1 Cor. 2:4-5).

Blind Right Eye and Left Eye Going Blind Completely Healed

I will never forget all the great miracles that God has performed since He called me and Aimee into the healing ministry. During the pastors' conference, a woman totally blind in her right eye and partially blind in her left eye was present. She had to be led around because of the blindness. After seeing the nine-year-old boy's deaf right ear opened, her faith was strengthened. She came forward for prayer, believing to receive sight.

I laid hands on her in the name of Jesus and commanded sight to be restored. Immediately following the prayer of faith, she was healed. God restored her vision before everyone's eyes. The crowd began to praise God for performing such an awesome miracle. She demonstrated her healing by following me. She raised the same amount of fingers as I raised.

> Jesus answered and said unto him, what wilt thou that I should do unto thee? The blind man said unto him, Lord, that I might receive my sight. And Jesus said unto him, Go thy way; thy faith hath made thee whole. And immediately he received his sight, and followed Jesus in the way (Mark 10:51-52).

Grapefruit-Sized Tumor Disappeared

In this same service, an elderly woman came forward for prayer, believing that God would heal the tumor in her stomach. This tumor was so big, this woman looked like she was pregnant. I laid my hands on that tumor and cursed it in the name of Jesus. The healing anointing began to flow into that tumor.

After the laying on of hands, within about five minutes, the tumor began to shrink. The tumor shrunk all the way down to about two inches in diameter. By the next day, it had completely vanished. Glory be to God. Jesus is alive. She gave glory to God for healing her body and removing the tumor. "...He shewed himself alive after his passion by many infallible proofs, being seen of them forty days, and speaking of the things pertaining to the kingdom of God…" (Acts 1:3).

Cancer in the Leg Cured

In one of the pastors' conferences, the Lord's power was present to heal His people. I instructed people to place their hands on the part of their body where they wanted God to heal them. I prayed the prayer of faith without laying hands on anyone. The healing anointing began to manifest and heal people everywhere. Many miracles took place. We had people come forward to testify what God had done.

A young man, seventeen years old, suffered with cancer in his leg since the age of five. He came to the platform to tell what God had done. During the prayer of faith, the cancer that was eating up his leg was completely healed. He demonstrated his healing by slapping his hands on that leg over and over. He lifted up his pants leg for everyone to see the scars the cancer had left. Every trace of pain had disappeared and he was totally healed. Praise God! The atmosphere was charged with faith.

Intestines Completely Healed

One of the outstanding miracles that took place when Aimee preached the Gospel and prayed for the sick occurred in the life of a woman. God's power manifested real strong. After instructing people to place their hands on the part of their body where they needed a miracle, the prayer of faith was prayed. Sickness and disease were commanded to go in the name of Jesus. The healing anointing of the Holy Ghost began to move, healing many in the congregation.

Present in that service was a woman who, for five years, whenever she used the restroom, her intestines would begin to come out of her body. Every time this happened, she would push her intestines back into her body with her hand. She testified that, after the prayer of faith was prayed, she had to go and check it. For the first time in five years, her intestines did not come out when she went to the restroom. She was totally healed by the power of the Holy Ghost. As a result of this miracle of healing, this lady gave her heart to Jesus. "And a great multitude followed him, because they saw his miracles which he did on them that were diseased" (John 6:2).

Woman's Foot Healed

Another outstanding miracle took place among the many miracles that broke out. A woman who was unable to walk without the aid of a big stick was healed. We took her walking stick from her and she walked. Praise God for the awesome miracles that He worked among His people. Many people gave their lives to Jesus because the miracles of healings proved Jesus resurrected. They knew that He was alive. "And with great power gave the apostles witness of the resurrection of the Lord Jesus: and great grace was upon them all" (Acts 4:33).

Broken Leg Healed

The pastors' conference took place in the morning and the miracle crusade took place at night. God's power always manifests as the Gospel is preached without compromise. A young boy who was run over by a motorbike suffered a broken leg and had been brought out to the crusade. During prayer for the sick, his broken leg was healed. He came onto the platform and ran, demonstrating that God had manifested a healing miracle on that leg. The crowd began to praise and magnify God for working such signs and wonders in their midst.

A Five-Year-Old Boy's Broken Arm Healed

In one of the services, a five-year-old with a broken arm was brought to the crusade to receive a miracle. After the prayer of faith for healing took place, his broken arm had been completely healed.

He was brought to the platform. My wife raised his arm up and down to demonstrate to the great crowd that the boy was healed. The crowd praised God. You never get tired of seeing God perform healing miracles.

Paralyzed Right Hand Healed

A woman suffered from a car wreck that paralyzed her right hand. She came to the miracle services, believing God to heal her hand. Her right hand was open stiff and she could not close it. During the prayer for the sick, God touched her hand. In an instant, it was completely healed and restored to normal. She lifted her hand, opening and closing her fist. She could not wait to go home to wash dishes. God restored her hand.

> And when he had looked round about on them with anger, being grieved for the hardness of their hearts, he saith unto the man, Stretch forth thine hand. And he stretched it out: and his hand was restored whole as the other (Mark 3:5).

Paralyzed Infant Walks

During the testimony part of the miracle crusade, a mom brought her two-year-old baby to the platform. She testified that her baby was paralyzed. As the prayer of faith for the sick was prayed, the baby began walking for the first time. Jesus showed Himself alive by notable miracles.

Demoniac of the Town Set Free

The greatest miracle of all is the saving of the soul. During the crusade, a demon-possessed man came. Many Christians were afraid of this man. He was in his twenties. His mother was also at the crusade, believing God to set him free. He had been in that condition for two entire years. His mother had taken him to many witch doctors to cure her son, but to no avail. Isn't it amazing what people will do when there is no one present walking in God's power? He was very popular in the town because he was extremely wild and full of fury. On this particular night, while preaching the Gospel of Jesus, the Holy Ghost moved mightily.

As I preached the Word of God, the Holy Ghost spoke to me and said, "Command every demon to leave now." I obeyed and there was a great breakthrough. After obeying the Holy Ghost, I felt led to make the altar call for salvation. To everyone's amazement, the young man came forward. I rushed over to where he was and looked him straight into his eyes. He looked humble as a lamb. He had one of the most tender looks that I have ever seen. I said, "What do you want?" He answered and said, "I want to give my life to Jesus." I led him in the prayer of salvation and he was gloriously saved.

Guess what happened next! The multitude that saw what happened broke out into a praise that was almost beyond explanation. Someone offered to give him a haircut and we gave him many clothes. His mother wept and rejoiced because God had answered her prayer. My life went to another level in God when this miracle took place. "And they come to Jesus, and see him that was possessed with the devil, and had the legion, sitting, and clothed, and in his right mind: and they were afraid" (Mark 5:15).

God performed many more miracles than we have recorded in this book.

> And there are also many other things which Jesus did, the which, if they should be written every one, I suppose that even the world itself could not contain the books that should be written. Amen (John 21:25).

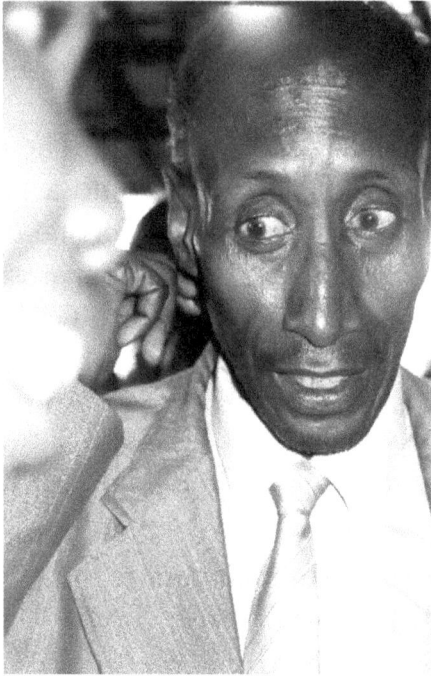

**This pastor had neck and back pain for years.
He came to Evangelists Sean and Aimee Pinder's Pastors'
Conference and was totally healed.**

This pastor's wife's baby was in the hospital, near death with a high fever. Evangelist Sean spoke the word to her husband, and the baby was healed and released from the hospital in the same hour.

Due to an accident, this lady's left hand was paralyzed. After the power of God fell, she demonstrated her ability to flex her hand freely.

To Book Evangelists Sean and Aimee Pinder for Miracle Services in your Church or Conference, send your emails to info@miraclehealingcenter.net.

You may also visit us online at www.miraclehealingcenter.net

www.ingramcontent.com/pod-product-compliance
Lightning Source LLC
Chambersburg PA
CBHW071127090426
42736CB00012B/2037